Dedicated to my grandchildren

Addison Lambert

And

Olivia-Lane Lambert

With Love,

Sissy

ISBN # 978-0-9800108-0-0

Kate's Funny Shoes

By Sims Lambert

Illustrated by Branden Ashley Chapin

I am so excited
My school begins today
I am 6 years old, a big girl now
My Mom and Dad both say

I am a little scared to go today
All the new friends I will meet
I hope they really like me and
Don't notice my funny feet

My hair is curled and pretty
My blouse is tied with bows
But oh my shoes are big and ugly
I hope nobody knows

My Mom says not to worry
We'll dress up with ribbons and bows
My Daddy says I'm a princess
From my head down to my toes

My teacher's name is Miss Ruthie
She is pretty and so kind
She took my hand and showed me
The desk that would be mine

I met the other children and
Told them my name was Kate
So far they had not noticed
I was slow and a little late

Soon it was time for recess
And we decided to play ball
"Hurry up Kate" they said to me
"Throw it back" but I would fall

"I do not want you on my team"
Billy said as we went in
"If we had you playing on our side
We would never, never win"

Sally and Jenny said to me
"Where in the world did you get your shoes?
Ours are pink and pretty
But yours will never do"

I covered my eyes and started to cry
But Anna said to me
"It's all right Kate they're just mean
We can be friends
You'll see"

I cried and cried and cried all night
Do I have to go back to school?
But Mom and Dad both hugged me
And said it was the rule

So I went back the very next day
Miss Ruthie was waiting there
She had a surprise to tell us all
Now she would tell us where

The Fair had come to town that day
And our class was asked to show
All the artwork we had made at school
To the judges who would come and go

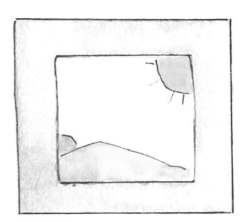

If our class could win 1st prize
We would ride all the rides that day
With ice cream, cookies, and fun
things to do
We could have a holiday

"I do not like to draw" Billy said
"I'd rather play ball at school"
Jenny and Sally said their shoes lost a bow
And they would not look cool

Anna spoke up and said
"My friend Kate can draw the best of all
If she could win the prize for us
We could have a ball

Billy can hold her hand to walk
Sally and Jenny can dress her shoes
Kate can help us draw
And we would never lose"

Sally and Jenny dressed up Kate's shoes
Billy helped her walk
Kate went around to each one's desk
To help them draw with chalk

We all have things we do the best
And some things we can't do at all
But altogether we are a team
And we will never fall

Guess what?

We won 1st prize at the fair
Together we had the best show
We all had so much fun that day
It was sad when we had to go

Today is the best day I have ever had
My new friends were so sweet
I could not run and jump like them
But they did not notice...
My funny feet

If this book could teach just
One child to be more tolerant...

Printed in the United States
93558LV00002B

9780980010800